SITTING BULL

SIOUX WAR CHIEF

CHRIS HAYHURST

rosen central
Primary Source™

The Rosen Publishing Group, Inc., New York

Published in 2004 by The Rosen Publishing Group, Inc.
29 East 21st Street, New York, NY 10010

Library of Congress Cataloging-in-Publication Data

Hayhurst, Chris.
Sitting Bull / Chris Hayhurst.— 1st ed.
    p. cm. — (Primary sources of famous people in American history)
Summary: A biography of the Sioux chief who worked to maintain the rights of Native American people and who led the defeat of General Custer at the Little Bighorn in 1876.
Includes bibliographical references and index.
ISBN 0-8239-4120-5 (lib. bdg.)
ISBN 0-8239-4192-2 (pbk. bdg.)
6-pack ISBN 0-8239-4319-4
1. Sitting Bull, 1834?-1890—Juvenile literature. 2. Dakota Indians—Biography—Juvenile literature. 3. Hunkpapa Indians—Biography—Juvenile literature. [1. Sitting Bull, 1834?-1890. 2. Dakota Indians—Biography. 3. Hunkpapa Indians—Biography. 4. Indians of North America—Great Plains—Biography. 5. Kings, queens, rulers, etc.]
I. Title. II. Series.
E99.D1 S584 2003
978.004'9752'0092—dc21

2002153671

Manufactured in the United States of America

Photo credits: cover (X-33835), pp. 4 (X-31668), 5 (B-74), 21 (X-33793), 24 (B-348), 25 (B-750), 26 (B-793A) Denver Public Library, Western History Collection; pp. 7 (top), 11, 19 © Hulton/Archive/Getty Images; p. 7 (bottom) South Dakota State Archives; p. 8 © Geoffrey Clements/Corbis; p. 9 Smithsonian American Art Museum, Washington, D.C./Art Resource, NY; pp. 12, 16 Werner Forman/Art Resource, NY; pp. 13, 18 © North Wind Picture Archives; p. 14 © Christie's Images/Corbis; p. 15 © Stapleton Collection/Corbis; p. 17 © Bettmann/Corbis; pp. 22, 28 Library of Congress Prints and Photographs Division; p. 23 (top) The Stapleton Collection/The Bridgeman Art Library; p. 23 (bottom) Whitney Gallery of Western Art, Cody, Wyoming/The Bridgeman Art Library; p. 27 © Corbis; p. 29 © Dave G. Houser/Corbis.

Designer: Thomas Forget; Photo Researcher: Rebecca Anguin-Cohen

CONTENTS

CHAPTER 1	A Young Boy	4
CHAPTER 2	The Warrior	12
CHAPTER 3	The Leader	18
CHAPTER 4	War	24
	Timeline	30
	Glossary	31
	Web Sites	31
	Primary Source Image List	31
	Index	32

1 A YOUNG BOY

The year was 1831. Along the Grand River in present-day South Dakota, a Native American woman was giving birth. The father, a Lakota Sioux warrior, stood nearby. The baby was born. His parents named him Jumping Badger.

Two Lakota Sioux women sit in front of their tepees with bundles of kindling wood. The Sioux were nomadic people and camped wherever the buffalo were.

This studio photograph of Sitting Bull was taken in the 1880s after the Battle of the Little Bighorn and after he had surrendered to the U.S. Army.

Jumping Badger seemed different from other children in the Hunkpapa Lakota tribe. He moved slowly and thought deeply before acting. Soon he was given the nickname Hunkesni, which means "slow." But Hunkesni was certainly not slow. As he grew up, he was quick to master important skills.

DID YOU KNOW?

The name given to Sitting Bull, Tatanka Iyotanka, was chosen to reflect his firmness and courage. It describes a buffalo sitting on its haunches and refusing to move.

A young Native American sits on his horse. American Indian men were taught to ride well at an early age. Below, a map of the Dakota Territory. The Black Hills are in the western part of the territory.

One of the skills Hunkesni mastered was hunting. The Hunkpapa tribe and all the Lakota people hunted buffalo for food. The great animal was also a source of clothing, shelter, and bedding. Hunting buffalo was a way of life for the Lakota. Hunkesni killed his first buffalo at the age of ten.

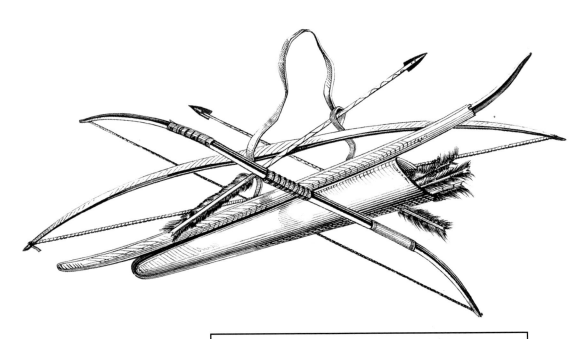

A drawing of Sioux Indian bows, arrows, and a quiver. The bow and arrow were very important in a community that hunted for its food.

A depiction of a buffalo hunt on the
prairie by the artist John M. Stanley
(1814–1872)

The buffalo was so important to the Lakota that it often led them to war. Other Native American tribes also hunted buffalo. Sometimes their hunting grounds overlapped. The tribes fought each other for the buffalo and the land where they lived. It was important for Lakota boys to learn to fight.

THE BUFFALO

Native Americans obtained almost everything they needed from the buffalo. It fed them. It provided skins for clothing and tepees. Its sinews were used to make string for arrows.

A sketch of a Native American
village by the artist George Catlin
(1796–1872). On the right, buffalo
hides are being cleaned and dried.

2 THE WARRIOR

It was 1845. Hunkesni and a group of Lakota warriors arrived at a river and found a band of Crow warriors by the water. Hunkesni, leading the way, was the first Lakota to strike. He knocked a Crow off his horse. Within minutes, almost all the Crow warriors were dead.

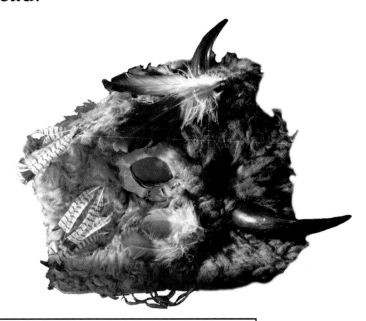

Sioux pony masks were worn by horses at Native American dances and ceremonies to show the importance of their owners.

A mounted Native American warrior examines the enemy dead after a skirmish between different tribes.

At a special ceremony, Hunkesni's father congratulated his son for his bravery. Then, to honor his becoming a man, he gave him his name. Hunkesni would now be known as Tatanka Iyotanka—Sitting Bull.

A Sioux warrior's shirt. Such shirts were dyed with local pigments and adorned with quill work and hair.

This picture of dancing, by the Native American artist Amos Bad Heart Buffalo, was painted sometime around 1890.

In 1857, Sitting Bull was named war chief of the Hunkpapa tribe. He was also recognized as a holy man, or Wichasha Wakan.

The Hunkpapa believed Sitting Bull had great spiritual powers. A great leader was exactly what they needed. A new threat—far greater than the Crow—was upon them.

The eagle feather warbonnet worn by Sioux chiefs. Sitting Bull is pictured wearing such a bonnet on page 5.

Hunters shoot buffalo that seem to block the passage of a train. Any excuse was used to kill buffalo because Native Americans depended on them for food.

3 THE LEADER

Sitting Bull had seen white people all his life. Sometimes the whites and the Lakota would meet to trade. Other times they would fight. The real goal of the whites was gold and new territory. They felt they had a right to Native American land.

These Native Americans are trading buffalo hides for gunpowder, sugar, tea, and other goods at the trading post.

Many easterners sympathized with Native Americans. In this magazine cartoon, Nelson Miles, responsible for the massacre at Wounded Knee, is depicted as profiting from his management of the reservations.

In 1868, the Lakota elected Sitting Bull leader of the entire tribe. Sitting Bull worked hard to unite his people. In the winter of 1876, soldiers attacked and destroyed a Native American camp. They forced the surviving Native Americans out into the cold. Sitting Bull saw this as an act of war.

THE BLACK HILLS BECOME VALUABLE

Sitting Bull and the Lakota Sioux were told to move to reservations because gold had been discovered on their land. The expedition that made the discovery was led by George Armstrong Custer.

Sitting Bull addresses his followers
and calls for resistance against U.S.
demands that his people move out of
the Black Hills.

On June 25, 1876, Major General George Armstrong Custer led his troops in an attack on the Lakota people. But Custer and his men were outnumbered. The Lakota, led by Sitting Bull, killed Custer and nearly all his men. But the U.S. Army kept attacking the Lakota and wore them down. One by one the Lakota tribes surrendered. Sitting Bull had to give in.

A photograph of Major General George Armstrong Custer. His reckless behavior won battles during the Civil War but led him to disaster at the Little Bighorn.

Two views of the Battle of the Little Bighorn. Above, the retreat of Major Reno's command by the Native American artist Amos Bad Heart Buffalo. Below, the grandly heroic painting of Custer's last stand by Edgar Paxton.

Sitting Bull and his tribe were sent to Standing Rock Reservation. The reservation was run by the U.S. government.

One day, members of the U.S. government came to Sitting Bull's reservation to explain that parts of the reservation would now be open to whites. Sitting Bull was angry.

A studio portrait of Sitting Bull and William "Buffalo Bill" Cody, taken in 1885. Sitting Bull briefly worked with Cody in his Wild West Show before returning to Sioux territory.

A photograph of one of Sitting Bull's trials at the Indian Agency on the Standing Rock Reservation, where he was accused of urging various tribes to resist white demands

The Lakota began performing a sacred ceremony called the Ghost Dance. They thought the dance would rid their land of white people forever and bring back the traditional way of life. American soldiers quickly forbade the Ghost Dance, but the Native Americans danced anyway.

A photograph of Sitting Bull's two wives and daughters, taken sometime in the 1880s

Sioux Indians perform the Ghost Dance, part of a new religious cult that taught the Sioux that the white man's bullets could not kill them.

Back at Standing Rock Reservation, the government feared that Sitting Bull would bring the Ghost Dance to his people. On December 15, 1890, they sent Native American policemen to Sitting Bull's home to arrest him. They dragged him outside. In the confusion, a fight erupted. Shots rang out. Sitting Bull was dead.

Sitting Bull's grave site, near Mobridge, South Dakota. By the time of his death, the Indian Wars were over, and most tribes were confined to reservations.

The monument to Sitting Bull was built near his grave site outside of Mobridge, South Dakota.

TIMELINE

1831—Sitting Bull is born near the Grand River.

1845—Sitting Bull fights his first battle and is honored by his tribe as a warrior.

1857—Sitting Bull is named war chief of the Hunkpapa Lakota Sioux.

1868—Sitting Bull is elected head chief of the Lakota Sioux.

1876—War begins between the Lakota Sioux and the United States Army.

1880s—Sitting Bull and his tribe are forced to live on a reservation.

1890—Sitting Bull is murdered as he is arrested by reservation police.

GLOSSARY

ceremony (SER-ih-moh-nee) A special celebration done on certain occasions.

chief (CHEEF) A leader of a Native American tribe or nation.

Hunkpapa (huhnk-pah-pah) A tribe of the Lakota Indians.

reservation (reh-zer-VAY-shun) An area of land set aside by the government for a special purpose.

warrior (WAR-ee-yur) One who goes into battle.

WEB SITES

Due to the changing nature of Internet links, the Rosen Publishing Group, Inc., has developed an online list of Web sites related to the subject of this book. This site is updated regularly. Please use this link to access the list:

http://www.rosenlinks.com/fpah/sbul

PRIMARY SOURCE IMAGE LIST

Page 4: Two Native American women, from a stereograph produced by Bailey, Dix, & Mead in 1882, now with the Denver Public Library.

Page 5: Photograph by David Francis Barry, 1880s, now with the Denver Public Library.

Page 7: A stereograph of a young Native American man on horseback. Below, a map of the Dakota Territory, 1880s, courtesy of the South Dakota Historical Society.

Page 8: Sioux Indian bows and arrows, drawn by Karl Bodmer in the 1830s.

Page 9: *Buffalo Hunt on the Southwestern Prairies*, by John M. Stanley, oil on canvas, 1845, now with the Smithsonian Institution.

Page 11: *An Indian Village*, by George Catlin (1796–1872).

Page 12: Pony mask, now with the Museum of the American Indian, Heye Foundation.

Page 13: Native American warrior, hand-colored engraving.

Page 14: Sioux warrior's shirt, photographed by Peter Harholdt in 1849.

Page 15: *Dance in Honor of the Warrior He Dog*, by Amos Bad Heart Buffalo, c. 1890.

Page 16: Eagle feather warbonnet, now with the Plains Indian Museum, Buffalo Bill Historical Center, Cody, Wyoming.

Page 17: *Shooting Buffalo*, from *Frank Leslie's Illustrated Newspaper*, June 3, 1871, now with the Library of Congress.

Page 19: "Indian Agent," 1890.

Page 21: *Sitting Bull Addresses His Followers*, from *Kelsey's History of the Wild West*, published between 1880 and 1890.

Page 22: George Armstrong Custer, photographed by Matthew Brady before 1865, now with the Library of Congress.

Page 23: *The Retreat of Major Reno's Command* by Amos Bad Heart Buffalo (1869–1913), *Custer's Last Stand* by Edgar Paxton (1852–1915)

Page 24: Sitting Bull and William Cody, photographed in 1885 by David Francis Barry, now with the Library of Congress.
Page 25: The Standing Rock Indian Reservation, photographed by David Francis Barry in 1886, now with the Library of Congress.
Page 26: Photograph of Sitting Bull's wives and daughters, taken by David Francis Barry in the 1880s, now with the Library of Congress.
Page 27: *Ghost Dance*, 1881.

INDEX

B
buffalo, 6, 8, 10

C
Crow Indians, 12, 16
Custer, George Armstrong, 20, 22

G
Ghost Dance, 26, 28
gold, 18, 20

H
Hunkesni, 6, 8, 12, 14
Hunkpapa Lakota tribe, 6, 8, 16
hunting, 8, 10

J
Jumping Badger, 4, 6

L
Lakota Sioux, 4, 8, 10, 12, 18, 20, 22, 26

R
reservations, 20, 24

S
Sitting Bull, 14, 16, 18, 20, 22, 24, 28
South Dakota, 4
Standing Rock Reservation, 24, 28

T
Tatanka Iyotanka, 6, 14
trade, 18

U
U.S. Army, 22

W
war, 10, 20
war chief, 16
white people, 18, 24
Wichasha Wakan, 16

ABOUT THE AUTHOR

Chris Hayhurst is an emergency medical technician, professional author, and journalist with more than a dozen books and hundreds of articles in print. He lives and works in Fort Collins, Colorado.